MEDIEVAL TAPESTRIES

COLORING BOOK

MARTY NOBLE

DOVER PUBLICATIONS, INC.
Mineola, New York

NOTE

Since medieval times, tapestries have been symbols of prosperity, status, and influence. Collections of these ornamental textiles were highly valued by monarchs and aristocrats, and these skilled weavings were often used as the spoils of war. Intricately designed tapestries were usually commissioned by royalty to decorate the rooms in medieval castles and manor houses. Not only used as decorative wall hangings, medieval tapestries also served some practical purposes as well, namely, for furniture, curtains, and insulation from drafts. Typical medieval tapestry designs consisted of religious themes; scenes of tournaments, battles, and hunts; allegorical scenes; and *mille fleurs* (characterized by backgrounds made up of thousands of tiny flowers). The most celebrated allegorical sequence is "The Lady with the Unicorn," a set of six panels representing each of the five senses as well as one entitled "A Mon Seul Desir." Five plates appear in full color on the covers.

Bibliographical Note

Medieval Tapestries Coloring Book is a new work, first published by Dover Publications, Inc., in 2004.

DOVER *Pictorial Archive* SERIES

This book belongs to the Dover Pictorial Archive Series. You may use the designs and illustrations for graphics and crafts applications, free and without special permission, provided that you include no more than four in the same publication or project. (For permission for additional use, please write to Permissions Department, Dover Publications, Inc., 31 East 2nd Street, Mineola, N.Y. 11501.)

However, republication or reproduction of any illustration by any other graphic service, whether it be in a book or in any other design resource, is strictly prohibited.

International Standard Book Number: 0-486-43686-1

Manufactured in the United States of America
Dover Publications, Inc., 31 East 2nd Street, Mineola, N.Y. 11501

Detail of chasuble (garment worn by priests for the celebration of the Eucharist), England, 1310–50.

"Death on His Pale Horse" tapestry, 1379.

"A Lady with a Dog and a Falcon," Franco-Flemish, 1400.

"Tree of Jesse" *(detail)* from a Rhinish wool hanging depicting Solomon, 1400s.

Image depicting the arms of Jean de Daillon and mille fleur motifs,
Flemish, late 15th century.

"The Griffin Protects the Lady" (detail), tapestry made in Basel, 1460.

"Rabbit Hunting with Ferrets," Franco-Flemish, 1460.

"History of Julius Caesar" *(detail)*, Flemish, 1465–70.

"History of Julius Caesar" *(detail)*, Flemish, 1465–70.

"A Lady and Two Gentlemen in a Rose Garden" *(detail)*, Southern Netherlands, 1450–55.

"The Start of the Hunt," first of the Seven Unicorns Tapestries,
Southern Netherlands, 1495–1505.

"The Unicorn is Found" *(detail)* from the series "The Hunt of the Unicorn as an Allegory of Passion," Southern Netherlands, 1480–90.

"The Unicorn in Captivity" from "The Hunt of the Unicorn as Lover,"
Southern Netherlands, 1495–1505.

13

"The Queen of Sheba before King Solomon," Upper Rhinish, 1490–1500.

Detail from a German fifteenth-century tapestry showing a game of cards.

"The Mystic Hunt of the Unicorn" (*detail*) from tapestry altar frontal, Swiss, 1480.

"The Mystic Hunt of the Unicorn" *(detail)* from tapestry altar frontal, Swiss, 1480.

"Sight," one of the tapestries from "The Lady with the Unicorn," a set of six tapestries, Southern Netherlands, 1480–90.

"Hearing" *(detail)* from "The Lady with the Unicorn," Southern Netherlands, 1480–90.

"Smell" *(detail)* from "The Lady with the Unicorn," Southern Netherlands, 1480–90.

"A Mon Seul Desir" (*detail*) from "The Lady with the Unicorn,"
Southern Netherlands, 1480–90.

"The Visit of the Gypsies" *(detail)*, Southern Netherlands, 1500–10.

"The Gaze of Narcissus," Franco-Flemish, 1500.

"Scenes from the Trojan War" (*detail*) from "The Arrival of Paris and Helen," Flemish, 1500.

"Scene at a Royal Court" *(detail)*, Flemish, 1500.

"The Combat of the Virtues and the Vices" *(detail)* from "The Redemption of Man"
series, Flemish, 1510–15.

"The Combat of the Virtues and the Vices" *(detail)* from "The Redemption of Man"
series, Flemish, 1510–15.

"The Combat of the Virtues and the Vices" (*detail*) from "The Redemption of Man" series, Flemish, 1510–15.

"The Creation and the Fall of Man" (*detail*) from "The Redemption of Man" series, Flemish, 1510–15.

29

"The Vices Attack Man" (*detail*) from "The Redemption of Man" series, Flemish, 1510–15.